T0380521

Poetry,
Oh Poetry
Maribelle Cooper Ash

Illustrations by
Brian Ortgies

Copyright © 2019 by Maribelle Cooper Ash. 797717

ISBN: Softcover   978-1-7960-4238-2
        EBook   978-1-7960-4237-5

All rights reserved. No part of this book may
be reproduced or transmitted in any form or by
any means, electronic or mechanical, including
photocopying, recording, or by any information storage
and retrieval system, without permission in writing from
the copyright owner.

The views expressed in this work are solely those of
the author and do not necessarily reflect the views of
the publisher, and the publisher hereby disclaims any
responsibility for them.

Print information available on the last page

Rev. date: 06/25/2019

To order additional copies of this book, contact:
Xlibris
1-888-795-4274
www.Xlibris.com
Orders@Xlibris.com

Poetry, Oh Poetry

Maribelle Cooper Ash

Contents

Jenny's Wedding

Have you ever fashioned a wedding
In a week and just one day?
Have you ordered a cake and flowers,
And an organist to play?

Have you ever picked out a wedding gown
The prettiest one in town?
Invited all the family
And your neighbors all around?

Have you given a daughter in marriage
In return, recieved a son?
Thanked the preacher for his service,
Thrown rice and shoes for fun?

If you haven't done it lately
But you know it could happen to you,
I hope it will be as lovely
As the wedding I've been thru.

Poetry, Oh Poetry

Poetry, Oh poetry
It's just my mind in motion
In rhythm with the things I think,
My ideas and my notions.

It's things to be remembered
As I pass along life's way,
That soon would be forgotten,
In the hustle of each day.

It doesn't take a minute,
It doesn't cost a dime,
To jot it down on paper,
In some simple little rhyme.

A Mother's Heart

God gave me a mother's heart
My home was to be his temple.
The task he set before me
Was just ordinary, and quite simple.

To be there when there was a need,
Sow love and kindness like a seed.

To instill the thought
At the end of each day.
That a better tomorrow
Is coming our way.

Picnic In The Snow

A picnic table scattered with seed
The birds flew down for a winter feed.

I watched from my window with glowing delight
The sun on the snow made it dazzling white.

It was hard to believe you could feed so many
With one quarter, two dimes, and a couple of pennies.

Extra, Extra...Read All About It

Up at five and he's on his way,
To deliver your paper to you today.

Though he's only eleven years old,
He does a good job; so I've been told.

Out in the dark, before the dawn,
A neatly rolled paper on every lawn.

It makes me proud that his job is well done,
For, your paper boy is my grandson.

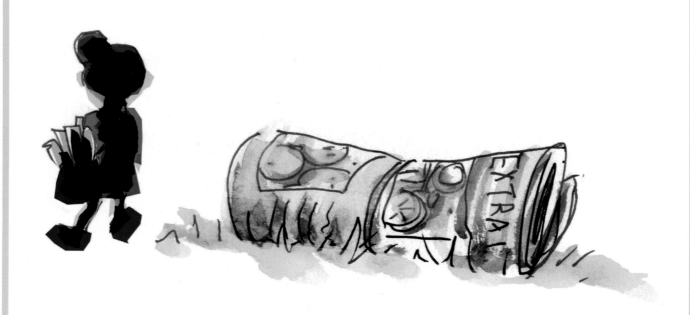

Snowflakes-Cornflakes

Our first snow of the winter came,
It was just the other day.
The snow and cold depressed me,
Till I heard my young son say

"Hey mom, look at the leaves",
They lay thick upon the ground,
"I think they look like Cornflakes,
With sugar sprinkled round".

Wounded Dove

The wounded dove soared gently
Into a higher flight.
Then disappeared completely
In Heaven's holy light.

Regret

Death imparts a knowledge that nothing else can teach,
When you have lost a loved one beyond all life and reach.

For suddenly you realize the error of your ways,
You could have been much better in a thousand little ways.

Saturday's Chores

What did I do today?
I cooked a pot of beans.
Then made a big fruit salad,
And ironed a pair of jeans.

I ran the sweeper, burned the trash
Did dishes several times,
Washed out a load of towels and such,
And hung them on the line.

I swept the porch, shook out a rug,
And gave the dogs their chow.
My Saturday is almost gone,
I wonder where, not how.

Dreams N' Things

One night I woke up suddenly
And sat up straight in bed.
My heart was beating wildly
And my mind was full of dread.

"Don't move, don't move", I said
As Pa lay in quiet rest.
For, I saw a spider dangling
Just an inch above his chest.

Of course he was dumb-founded
And it scared him just a bit,
But there wasn't any spider
I was dreaming all of it.

Lincoln's Day

On visiting a grade school on Abe Lincoln's Day,
And viewing the portraits proud students displayed,

White shirt, bow tie, and dark beard all quite true,
But, were Mr. Lincoln's eyes really sky blue?

The Mouse Trap

A mouse that came to visit us was very hard to please,
Ignored the trap we set for him with fine, fresh longhorn cheese.

He didn't like the flour, the sugar, or the spread
Of peanut butter that we put upon a piece of bread.

You'll not believe what finally caught that ornery little bum,
T'was just a tiny little piece of purple bubble gum.

Road To '76

On the road to '76
Thru the past two hundred years
To the building of a nation
Born of blood, sweat, toil, and tears.

To the making of a people
American by name
From a melting pot of races
To a new, red-blooded strain.

We have reached this point in destiny
And our hopes and prayers shall be
That America stays beautiful
America stays free!

First Class Male

Here he comes walking down the street,
It's our very own mailman, and he can't be beat.

Dressed all in blue, and he wears it well,
The uniform of the United States Mail.

Now, don't send a sub, for he won't do,
For, Dan is our pick of the regulars too!

There's a pretty good reason we chose this one,
He's not only our mailman, he's our son!!

Jack

Great sadness and deep sorrow have come to us today,
With the passing of a loved one that lived so far away.

A brother who was sweet, and kind, and loved by one and all,
Whose eyes now closed in slumber does not see our teardrops fall.

Compassion was the gift he gave to those whose need was great,
The gift he carries with him now, through Heaven's open gate.

The Last Blessing

Softly he came and slipped away
On a Sunday morning near the first of May.

In from his garden, he came to rest,
To his knees he sank, he was truly blessed.

On a sick bed he never had to lay,
Softly he came and slipped away.

The Wind Chimes

I hear the wind chimes tinkling,
On the porch outside my door.
Some think the wind has stirred them,
But it's Momma home once more.

It is her gentle spirit telling me she's near,
With the tinkling of the wind chimes,
As they ring so soft and clear.

They were the last thing that I gave her,
Just a tiny gift, it's true.
But I said "Mom, when you hear them
You will know I think of you".

Someday when time has eased the pain,
When I hear them, I will smile again.

Mom's An Angel Now

Good morning to you Momma,
And how are you today?
Beguiling all the angels,
In your own sweet, loving way.

Keeping rather busy
Just as you did on earth,
A kind word here, a good deed there,
Don't angels need some mirth?

You know we miss you Momma,
But we can't stay sad and blue.
For the sweetest mom from here on earth,
Is loved in Heaven too!

Put On Your Old Grey Bonnet With The Soccer Emblem On It

Green grows the grass on the soccer fields of Dover,
If you haven't been there yet, why don't you come on over.
Down in the valley, over the track,
Eight soccer fields running, back to back.

Good times, bad times, laughing and crying,
The winners keep winning, and the losers keep trying.
Fun for the young, and fun for the old,
Playing in the rain, and the heat, and the cold.

Put on your old grey bonnet with the soccer emblem on it,
And forget old Dobin and the shay,
We're going out to Dover and trample down the clover.
We're all playing soccer today.

All About Heaven

Most folks think Heaven is a place they will see,
After they've died it is where they will be.
But Heaven can also be found on this earth,
If you know how to value some things for their worth.

When spring rains fall softly in the middle of the night,
When the air through your window feels balmy and light,
When you know you can sleep late and enjoy such bliss,
Heaven can never be closer than this.

When there's soup in the pot when the weather is cold,
When you feel young at heart, though sometimes you feel old,
When that beautiful sunset you wouldn't dare miss,
Heaven can never be closer than this.

When the baby is bathed and all ready for bed,
And there's sweet scent of talcum on her sleepy head,
When she hugs you and gives you that last good night kiss.
Heaven can never be closer than this.

When thinking of Heaven don't look to the sky,
It's really much closer, it's very nearby.
It's in every day living where beauty exists,
Heaven can never be closer than this.

Give A Hug

There are many times a Mother wants to reach out and hug her son,
Not for anything he's said to her or anything he's done.

But just because she loves him in that very same old way,
That she did when he was little and would come inside from play.

For, once a boy becomes a man,
Those hugs aren't part of the social plan.

So, son if you should read this, then heed a mother's plea,
Just every now and then reach out, and give a hug to me.

Declaration Of Independence

I will not walk in your shadow,
I'll make one of my own,
I'll be my own true person,
I will not be a clone.

I'll see things as I see them,
Not as you would have me see,

In doing this if I oppose
Some others' point of view,
I still must be just what I am,
I will not be like you.

Work Of Art

Oh, those tiny little freckles upon my angel's face,
The sun shone down and sprinkled them each in its special place.

Beneath the eyes, across the nose and several on the chin,
A work of art by nature, when they're followed with a grin.

Mary Picky-Pants

Hello, I'm Mary Picky-pants
And why is that you say?
Because I wear polyester slacks
And even when they fray.

Although I'm rich in many ways,
My Scotch blood still shines through.
I simply cannot pitch my pants
Because of a pick or two.

A Mother's Way

A mother's way you see is this,
A little smile, a tender kiss.
To bend a twig that it may grow,
Into a kind and loving soul.

How beautiful this little child
That dreams in slumber sweet and mild,
How lucky me that I may share,
This bit of heaven lying there.

Sleeping beauty once again
Lies upon my palette thin,
Gazing at you through the night,
Visions of love's pure delight.

Sleeping beauty lying there
Dark lashes brushing cheeks so fair.
Those tiny little fingers touch
Soft, yellow blanket loved so much.

Oh, little one so sweet and dear,
Prince Charming must wait several years!

Lullaby Rock

Nana loved the classics,
She played them hours on end.
When little Evan came to stay,
She played them all for him.

She put her rocker in her room
And when his nap was due,
She put the classics on to play
And he enjoyed them too!

It is almost unbelievable
And hard to understand,
She could rock that baby sound asleep,
To the beat of the Can-Can.

If I were King

If I were King, here's what I'd say,
Kids, there'll be no school today.
Since I'm not King, but just a fool,
Guess I'd better go to school.

Bullfrogs At Church

Bullfrogs never go to church,
But I know one that did.
I took one in a bucket,
When I was just a kid.

Centennial plans were in full sway,
With a costume contest on that day.
Ma dressed me in old-fashioned clothes,
Just like Tom Sawyer I suppose.

At the Presbyterian Church we were all to meet,
Everyone entered and took a seat.
I didn't win a prize that day, but I had lots of fun
When that frog sprang from my bucket, and made the ladies run.

He was quite a whopper and quite a hopper,
But there were other places that he would rather be,
So, I went down to the river, and set that bullfrog free!

Who Put the Q
In Quapaw?

Who put the Q in Quapaw
On the water tank so high?

Just noticed it the other day
As I was passing by.

Now, they say heights make you dizzy
And can give you quite a fright.

Maybe that's why the Q in Quapaw
Is crossed on the left, not right.

Amy's Day

What did I do today?
Not much that you can see.
Today's the day that Amy came,
To stay awhile with me.

We listened to some records,
And danced around the room.
Went out and picked some flowers,
Bright Jonquils in full bloom.

We had some lunch, then rocked awhile,
She sat upon my lap.
We got so dog-gone sleepy,
We just had to have a nap.

The day passed by so quickly
My work was left undone.
But grandma and grand-daughter
Just had to have some fun.

First Bloom

She came in early spring time.
It snowed the night before.
The winds of March blew strong, and cold,
Snow flurries that they bore.

By early morn the sun peeped thru,
And with it's golden ray,
She came to warm and brighten,
Our lives upon that day.

She was the first of several blooms,
In our garden of God's plan.
We took her home to raise and love,
And called her Mischa Ann.

Sixth Sense

There are five senses known to man
But I'll add one more to the master plan.

First, there's touch, like in velvet clothes,
Then, there's one in smell, when you sniff a rose.

It's your sense of sight, when you see blue sky,
And your sense of taste, when you're eating pie.

There's the one you hear, when children sing,
And the TV blares, and the doorbell rings.

But the one that counts, when you're feeling blue,
It's your sense of humor, that pulls you thru.

The Shortest Span

My glass reflected wrinkles,
Yet, I just had to grin.
The kids were worried about the zits,
Appearing on their skin.

If I could just convince them
Their worries were quite small.
And the time from zits to wrinkles,
Is the shortest span of all!!

Last Dance

Just toss my ashes to the wind,
Watch them swirl and dance around.
They may blow all to pieces,
Or they may float to the ground.

Just toss my ashes to the wind,
Far better place to be,
Than underneath the cold, dark earth
For all eternity.

A Poem For Grant

"Will you write a poem for me?"
My young grandson said today.

Of course I will my honey,
Now let's see, what will I say?

I'll say how really sweet you are
And good in every way,
And how much fun we always have
When we go out and play.

I'll write about our parties
Where we sit upon the floor,
And have Coke, and cheese, and crackers,
And you always ask for more.

I'll say how hard you hit the ball
When you are up at bat,
And how funny and how cute you look
When you wear Grandpa's hat.

I'll say how lucky that I am
To have a boy like you,
And hope that you will feel the same
About your Grandma, too!

Only Two

He's been into mischief
Off and on all day,
Right under your feet
With his toys and his play.

He's tried your patience
But whatever you do,
Please just remember
He is only two!!

Jim

Jim swapped his tails
For a set of wings,

Now, with beautiful music
The heavens ring.

Goodbye Stapleton

Goodbye Stapleton, its graduation day,
And we must close the doors on you,
And go a different way.

We only hope the open doors
That we will be venturing through,
Will share their wisdom, friends, and fun
As we have shared with you.

Though childhood days go quickly past
And school days soon are done,
Most lasting of our memories dear,
Will be of Stapleton!

Stapleton Grade School

My mother thinks that it's quite fun
To write a poem or two.
And so she wrote this poem for me
Of school days tried and true.

And though I've been here six short years,
For her it's been much more,
For with four kids, one in, one out,
She's been here twenty four.

My Guardian Angel

See those clouds there in the sky,
Those angels sitting there,
My sister's the third one from the right,
The one with the short brown hair.

She's up there really, really high
But not too high you see,
For me to know that she's still here
Watching over me.

The Game

Some folks travel the wide world
In search of glory or fame,
To them it is exciting,
But to me, it's just a game.

For, my glory lies in a baby's eyes,
And I don't need any other,
For nothing compares
With the love that is shared
By a boy and his grandmother.

Looking Back

Hi! Mom, it's Mother's Day
And once again, I'll send,
A little message to you
With my loving thoughts tucked in.

Remember all the happy times
And funny things we did,
When you were still a young girl,
And I was just a kid.

Walking to the movies,
Each time we missed the bus,
Tying ribbons on my pigtails,
How I hated all that fuss.

The Sunday morning that I spent
All my offering money,
On candy, pop, and chewing gum,
You didn't think that funny.

They say that looking forward
Is the best thing that you can do.
But looking back is more fun,
When I'm looking back with you.

Going Back

We journeyed to the springs
Just below the mountains there,
A sadness swelled within me
And I felt a deep despair.

Fond memories of a bygone day,
When skies were fair and blue.
The mountains and the springs were there.
The one we missed was you.

Ignorance is Bliss

Ah, Youth, with all its restlessness
And age, with all its fears.
Ah, Youth, with all its ignorance
And age, with all its tears.

The nicest part of being young
A story often told,
Is the ignorance and unconcern,
Of ever being old.

Yet, with the old, the worst part,
Is a feeling deep within,
The realization of the fact
They'll not be young again.

The Royal Flush

Papa worked the night shift
And tried to sleep the day.
The kids were loud and noisy
With their voices and their play.

In the bathroom off Pa's bedroom,
The plumbing made a sound
Unlike any other in the household all around.

When we heard that noise,
Thru the house, there came a hush.
And everyone got quiet
When they heard the Royal Flush.

Reflection

On passing forty in high gear,
Reflecting on my past.
I ask myself "What have I done?"
In these years gone by so fast.

My family's almost all grown up
The youngest one is twelve.
I've learned to cook and sew a bit,
And manage fairly well.

I've planted flowers, mowed the yard,
Done many things but none too hard.

If I could go back twenty years
Relive this life or other,
I know that I'd still be content,
To be a Wife and Mother.

Little Baby Blue Eyes

Little baby blue eyes
How sweet and dear you are.
That little grin upon your face
Just sets my heart a-jar.

To hold you and to rock,
Gaze at you while you sleep.
Dark lashes brushing down upon
So fair and gentle cheek.

Little baby blue eyes
Mere words could never say,
The joy and love you bring to us
With every passing day.

Happy times,
remembered in rhymes

Printed in the United States
By Bookmasters